Through everything our worldwide [...] the luxury of middle ground. There isn't room for us to be lukewarm in our faith. It's time for us to wake up! There is not a better person to deliver this word than Pastor Lisa. I had the privilege of meeting her when I was a young girl, just beginning to grow and develop my beliefs. Pastor Lisa has been the most constant voice in my ear that remains to this day, encouraging me always to press on toward the goal in Christ. In my darkest seasons, it has repeatedly been Pastor Lisa to offer words of hope and light. This woman keeps it real! She is authentic and genuine with her love for the Lord and for His people. In writing this book, Pastor Lisa has prayed over you; she has prayed over these pages. The reason you are holding this book in your hands is because there is something inside of you that God wants to wake up! You have a mission and a call on your life, and as you allow Pastor Lisa into your heart, I promise you that mission will be awakened.

—*Britney McCartin, Campus Pastor, Motion Church*

If you know my mom, you know her heart is to awaken that one thing in your spirit that is keeping you from being empowered to RUN after all that God has for you! That's why I love her and why I connect so well with this book. I can confidently say she and God are my alarm clocks, telling me to "WAKE UP AND GO!" I believe every reader who picks up this book will become empowered and confident to wake and rise up! My prayer is that this book will encourage you as it did me.

—*Rebekah Kai, Director, Pound for Pound Enterprise*

Every female on this planet should read this God-inspired message! In this compelling and thought-provoking book, *Wake Up!*, you can feel God's heart through Pastor Lisa Kai. It's a call to action to women everywhere to arise and take hold of the power God has given them. Let Pastor Lisa teach you how to operate in the power of God's grace, embrace strength, discover your purpose, walk in freedom, and bring change in the world.

—*Evie R. Carranza, Arise Women's Director, Inspire Church*

The authenticity, authority, and punch of humor Pastor Lisa reveals in her book, *Wake Up!*, are undeniably empowering. She knows who she is and whose she is and desires for every reader to walk in that freedom also. This narrative is a resuscitative call to revival: an awakening! In a world that has fallen into a spiritual coma, Lisa's voice echoes off the pages a powerful and pivotal truth, full of love and a sense of urgency. It will cause you to "Wake Up" and walk out HIS purpose in and through you.

—*Heidi Fowler, Mrs. Hawai'i America 2018,*
Owner, Breathe Hawai'i

YES! YES! YES! Lisa's "tell it like it is" delivery once again reminds me to snap out of my tomorrow mindset. This book is just what I needed transitioning from active-duty military to being a full-time warrior in the Army of the Lord! Lisa genuinely desires for each of us to realize our full potential and walk into everything God has planned for our lives. Her loving "spiritual shaking" has freed me from shrinking back. I'M UP!

—*Angela Rutledge, Retired U.S. Air Force Officer*

wake up!

The alarm is sounding on your life!

lisa kai

DREAM
RELEASER
ENTERPRISES

DEDICATION

*Every word written in this book is dedicated to
all the women who have attended previous Arise
Conferences in Hawai'i. I still remember the day God
asked me to lead the women of Inspire Church and
help them fulfill their God-given potential. This book
is a reminder to women everywhere to stay awake,
to not be complacent, and to know who you are in
Christ. So, ladies, thank you for keeping me awake!*

table of contents

Dedication v

Introduction: A Word for This Season 13

01. She Wakes UP 19

02. She Realizes Who She Is 37

03. She Gets Things Done! 53

04. She is Focused and Fierce 67

05. She Uses Her Voice 81

Conclusion: She's Yielded to God's Spirit 101

FOREWORD

If you know anything about my friend Lisa Kai, then you know she is a woman who doesn't play. She is a straight shooter; I would even respectfully call her straight-up "gangsta." She says what she means and means what she says. Yet, she is so tender—like a mama bear warning her children out of great love and concern for them not to miss the mark. The words on these pages are convicting and convincing. I am honored to write this foreword.

Allow me to be the first one to declare that her new book, *WAKE UP!*, is more than a book; it's a word in season, a message for the masses. With eyes wide open, I urge everyone called by His name to read this prophetic book. Her words are neither minced, nor is there space wasted, and this book is definitely true to its name.

The message on every page has a voice, a much-needed voice, and it couldn't have come at a better time. The revelation Lisa delivers is compelling. It's as though she is standing by our bedside, sounding the alarm while simultaneously dousing us with a bowl of iced water, waking us out of our spiritual stupor. The truth that is shared, anointed by the Holy Spirit, is urging us to throw off the hypnotic covers of complacency while exposing the strides that the enemy has taken in this season. She is pleading with us to become aware of all the time that has been lost while we've had our hand on the snooze button.

As you continue to read, spiritual blinders seem to melt away chapter by chapter. A soberness seems to catapult us, jolting us out of the spiritual coma of complacency that we might have found ourselves in.

But *Wake Up!* doesn't leave us standing by our bedside. It compels us to move forward and fan into flame the gifts that God has placed within us, which are so needed in this hour. It makes us wonder why we ever left our post and why we have gone into spiritual hibernation while the clock of Jesus' return is ticking.

This book inspires our faith and propels us to stand up and let the enemy of our soul know that his days are short. It makes us realize that the enemy who has pushed us into a corner has done so because he is deathly afraid of a believer who is determined to follow Him. He is fearful of a believer who will not relent but will pick up every spiritual weapon in their God-given arsenal and fight the good fight of faith.

Lisa lets us understand that regardless of this season of shutdown, we, as the body of Christ, are neither shut down nor shut out of our purpose.

So, get ready! This is war! Once we've been awakened, we will never desire to go back and sleep on the job. The Holy Spirit will baptize us with fresh boldness and courage, empowering us all to go the distance.

Well done, Lisa!

—Pastor Maria Durso

Overseer Saints Church

Author of *From Your Head To Your Heart* and *Ageless*

Conference Speaker

INTRODUCTION:
A WORD FOR THIS SEASON

I began writing this book in 2020 at a time when the world had been thrust into a global pandemic because of COVID-19, a virus that completely caught everyone off guard. No one could have possibly predicted that this pandemic would wreak havoc on every aspect of our lives—from the shutdown of schools . . . to mask mandates every time you leave your house . . . to an inability to enjoy meals with friends at your favorite restaurant. With the Safe Access Oʻahu program, anyone entering Oʻahu restaurants, gyms, and other establishments must now show proof of vaccination or a negative COVID test. Without either, customers can no longer work out or dine indoors with family and friends.

I truly believe there is a spirit attached to this virus. The enemy is using COVID to cause spiritual blindness and confusion, holding people hostage through fear and control. Government shutdowns and mandatory COVID vaccinations have resulted in many families struggling financially because of job loss or decreased wages. Others are suffering emotionally because of COVID's social isolation or the stress of homeschooling their children, something they promised themselves they would never do. Fear continues to grip the nation as so many have lost their battle with the virus, and new, more infectious variants threaten to throw us back into more restrictive mandates. Life is not the same anymore, and people are trying to adjust to a new normal. I am one of those people. As our lives changed, Mike and I were compelled to pray more than ever before against fear. To combat fear from pushing us into wrong actions or freezing us into inaction, we reminded ourselves of Isaiah 41:10 (ESV):

> *"Fear not for I am with you. Do not be*
> *dismayed for I am your God."*

Satan pounced on the opportunity to use this virus in an attempt to keep us from moving forward. His desire was to shut the church down and keep people from meeting with one another, so we would become isolated. I have news for the enemy: the CHURCH WILL ALWAYS PREVAIL because the church is not a building; it is God's people. How did the church respond to the schemes of the enemy? We refused to let Satan have the victory. We enlarged God's Kingdom. We developed creative ways to meet safely in-person and online. We established new small groups so that more people from all over the world could feel a sense of connection and closeness despite being distanced.

As we look back on 2020, it is clear that we were definitely living in unprecedented times, with the end of the pandemic nowhere to be seen. Despite receiving gloomy news day after day, I can say without hesitation that God is still on the throne, and He is in control no matter what our eyes may see. God will wipe away this virus and continue to bring peace and comfort to our hearts as we continue to trust in Him. I have sensed that the enemy has been working overtime during this pandemic: using distractions, fear and separation to keep us unaware of what God is doing here on earth. What the enemy does not realize is that God shines His brightest during those times when the world seems the darkest, even during a pandemic! He is the Alpha and the Omega, the Beginning and the End, and He shines light into all darkness (Revelation 21:6-7, John 1:5). We shall not fear during these dark times because God's light never dims and certainly never goes out.

One of the most devastating consequences of the prolonged pandemic is that God's children have fallen asleep—asleep to our God-given potential, our purpose, and our God-sized assignments. We have allowed slumber to render our senses dull to what God is doing around us. Regardless of whether you are a new Christian or have been walking with Jesus for many years, you must guard against the danger of falling asleep, particularly during this incredible time of uncertainty. Even the disciples, who had spent over three years with Jesus 24/7, found themselves unable to stay awake shortly before the crucifixion.

Matthew 26:36-42 (NLT) describes the situation:

Then Jesus went with them to the olive grove called Gethsemane, and he said, "Sit here while I go over there to pray." He took Peter and Zebedee's two sons, James and John, and he became anguished and distressed. He told them, "My soul is crushed to the point of death. Stay here and keep watch with me."

He went on a little farther and bowed with his face to the ground, praying, "My Father! If it is possible, let this cup of suffering be taken away from me. Yet I want your will to be done, not mine."

Then he returned to the disciples and found them asleep. He said to Peter, "Couldn't you watch with me even one hour? Keep watch and pray so that you will not give in to temptation. For the spirit is willing, but the body is weak!" Then Jesus left them a second time and prayed, "My Father! If this cup cannot be taken away unless I drink it, your will be done."

When he returned to them again, he found them sleeping, for they couldn't keep their eyes open. Did you catch that? They could not keep their eyes open. Jesus was crushed with grief, but the disciples found themselves struggling to keep their eyes open for even one hour. It is no different today. The pandemic has lulled many of us to sleep. Now is the time to remain awake and alert, lest we fall prey to the tactics of the enemy who grows desperate with each passing day because he knows the day of the Lord's return is drawing closer. My prayer for you as you read this book is that you will not just wake up, but that you will remain wide awake to the enemy's attacks against you, your family, and the church. . . . NOT ON MY WATCH!

01.

SHE WAKES UP

Hey, YOU, WAKE UP! It's time for you, yes, YOU, to get up! How often have you had to say that to yourself as you struggle to get out of bed on Monday mornings? How many times have you had to wake up your children or your spouse when it is time to get ready for school or work because the clock is ticking and they are in danger of sleeping through the alarm … again? For the past twenty-plus years, this has probably been one of my most repeated phrases to my family—particularly to my husband who repeatedly snoozes his alarm to grab a few extra minutes of sleep. I get it. Sometimes we are so exhausted because of the hectic daily demands of work, family, and church that time seems to literally fly past us.

Did you know that many Americans only get between five to seven hours of sleep at night? My doctor stresses that we should be getting at least seven hours of sleep. No wonder people are so tired! A lack of sleep can interrupt our focus and mental acuity, adversely impacting our overall health and even work performance. I have been guilty of craving just an extra 10-30 minutes of sleep, especially on cold mornings when I can't seem to make myself wake up in my comfy bed. I catch one whiff of my pillow and find myself slowly sinking back into my 500-thread count sheets as I drift back into sleep.

As Christians, we can sometimes find ourselves in a pattern of snoozing when God sounds the alarm to wake up! It is not that we have necessarily fallen into a deep sleep, but we are unable to fully wake ourselves up to do everything God has called us to do. Has God been trying to tell you it is time to turn off the snooze button and wake up from your sleep?

When my children were little, I discovered the best way to lull them to sleep was to let them snuggle with their favorite blankets. My youngest daughter, Charis, who is not so little anymore, adored her Piglet blanket. I remember how Charis would often grab onto the soft, silky edge of the blanket as I put her down to bed. She became so attached to the blanket that she would not fall asleep without it. The question is: what causes us to fall asleep?

COMPLACENCY

Our enemy Satan is not only delighted when we hit snooze, but he also has a personalized blanket that is designed to lull us back to sleep. Perhaps the enemy has deceived you with the blanket of complacency that keeps you so comfortable you fail to walk obediently when God calls you to go deeper. Or could it be that you are holding so tightly to the blanket of security that the enemy has pulled over your eyes that you are unable to move past fear, failure, or unforgiveness and get up?

Did you know the name Satan in Hebrew means "the adversary"? What exactly is an adversary? The term adversary is defined as an enemy or someone who opposes and resists. You can be certain that the enemy will resist you every time you try to wake up. He is rather delighted if he can succeed in lulling you back to sleep because when you are snoozing, you cannot fulfill what God has called you to do. When we sink into our comfortable beds and pull the enemy's blanket up over our heads, we become oblivious to his schemes to steal, kill, and destroy all that we hold dear. We must be willing to pull back the blankets and open our spiritual eyes, so we can be continuously alert and aware of what is truly happening around us. I came across a post one day that read: "Be the kind of woman that when your feet hit the floor each morning the devil says, 'Oh Crap. She's UP!'" The moment I saw the post, something inside me awakened, almost as if the Holy Spirit was stirring me from my spiritual slumber.

It reminded me of the story of Lazarus, whom Jesus brought back to life from death in John 11. Lazarus lived in Bethany near Jerusalem with his sisters, Mary and Martha. One day, when Lazarus became ill, his sisters sent word to Jesus because they knew how much He loved their brother. Although Lazarus died before He arrived in Judea, Jesus recognized that God has the power to bring dead things back to life. Jesus turned to His disciples and declared in verse 11 (NIV):

"Our friend Lazarus has fallen asleep; but
I am going there to wake him up."

By the time Jesus arrived, all hope seemed lost. Lazarus had been in the tomb for four days. Upon seeing Mary and the Jews who had come to comfort the family weeping, Jesus was moved in spirit and deeply troubled and wept. When he reached the tomb where Lazarus had been laid to rest, Jesus requested that the stone at the entrance be removed. He called forth in a loud voice:

"Lazarus, come out!"

Immediately, Lazarus got up and came out of the tomb with his hands and feet still wrapped with strips of linen and a cloth around his face. What a sight that must have been! Imagine how Satan must have felt when the man he had presumed dead woke up and began to walk toward the calling Jesus?

Are you like Lazarus? Have you fallen into such a deep sleep with your covers pulled snugly over your head that the dreams and plans God has for your life appear to be dead? Like Lazarus, are your hands and feet bound because you have been caught in a perpetual cycle of hitting the snooze button? In the original Greek text, Jesus is referred to as *thanatou* or Jesus of the Dead meaning that He is Lord of both physical and spiritual death. It is interesting to note that the Greek word for sleep used in John 11, *hypnou*, means a spiritual sleep. Jesus wants us to wake up from our spiritual slumber, no matter how long we have been asleep, whether four days or four years. As I reflected on the post I had read, I realized that Jesus is calling each and every one of us to wake up from our spiritual slumber and come forth, just like Lazarus. What else causes us to fall asleep?

BUSYNESS

Have you been napping or slumbering when you should be rising from your sleep? If you feel like Satan has been targeting you because your snoozing has made you inactive, numb, and desensitized to what is going on in the spiritual realm, then keep reading. God placed a burning desire in my heart to share this message with you because many years ago, I, too, had fallen asleep for a season.

Like other wives and mothers, I was busy taking care of my husband and three children. You know how it is. The majority of your time is spent getting the kids ready for the day, driving them to and from school, preparing a healthy breakfast, snack, and dinner, then getting the children ready for bed, so you can wake up early the next morning and repeat the cycle. Of course, that does not include the time you spend taking care of your husband, if you know what I mean. I found myself exhausted by the end of the day, with little time for me to do anything other than my work at church. If we are not careful, we can become stuck as our daily routine goes on week after week. It is easy to get lost in the familiar pattern of everyday life, even with good things like taking care of your family, that you forget God has so many more opportunities for you to grow and find your purpose in life.

OVERFAMILIARITY

The last thing I believe that causes us to fall asleep is becoming too familiar with the moment. Let me explain. In Matthew 26:36-42, Peter was unable to stay awake when Jesus prayed in the Garden of Gethsemane. Perhaps it was because Peter became too comfortable with the routine of Jesus going off to pray and spending time alone with His Father. Maybe Peter allowed the familiar to lull him to sleep, making him ill-equipped to understand the gravity of the situation. Although Jesus was about to willingly sacrifice His life on the cross, could it be that Peter was unable to stay awake for even one hour because he thought it was just an ordinary night? A little sleep never hurt anyone, right? Wrong!

When we become too familiar with the routines of day-to-day living, we are in danger of closing our eyes to divine moments, God's sense of urgency, and opportunities to accomplish God-sized assignments. I have found myself hitting the snooze button time and time again as I snuggle comfortably under the blanket of mastering my daily routine. As I snoozed, I failed to realize that God has greater plans for me to make an impact in this world. In fact, I only realized I had been asleep when I met other women at a conference who were making a difference all because they had decided it was time to wake up.

I will always remember that God-appointed moment when I witnessed over ten thousand women in Australia worshiping and leaning into God's Word. I was attending my very first women's conference. It was the first time I had ever heard a woman preach. Overwhelmed by the Holy Spirit, I left there with a vision to establish a women's conference back home on O'ahu, just like the one I had experienced. I wanted the women of Hawai'i to find freedom from slumber and be fully awake to fulfill the calling on their lives.

Imagine the difference we can make in the world when God's people collectively say to one another, "Hey—Wake up! It's time to Get Up!" Just as Jesus called Lazarus to come forth out of his sleep, this phrase will become our rallying cry throughout the world. God has been waking people up from their slumber since biblical times, and it is no different today. Why did God impress on my heart the need to write this book? Because people like you and me have become inactive in our relationship with Jesus and desperately need a resurrection or resuscitation to wake us up from our sleep. Now is not the time to snooze, but the time to rise up and be about God's business.

OH CRAP! SHE'S UP!

Although the enemy is unable to force us into doing his will, he will attempt to keep us slumbering with our eyes closed to the things that God is doing in our lives or in the world. The Greek word for devil means "false accuser." The enemy not only tells lies, but he is also a master at making us feel guilt and shame. He uses it to intimidate us into cowering under our covers. The enemy delights in distraction. His tactic is to keep us preoccupied and engrossed in our day-to-day responsibilities to the point that we are misled into thinking we do not have time for Jesus. The enemy shudders at the thought of our waking up because that will mean we grow in our personal relationship with Jesus and plant our roots firmly in God's Word. As long as the enemy can keep you distant, comatose, and oblivious to your identity in Christ, he will succeed in his mission.

As I look back on my life, I can't help but feel anger toward Satan for blinding me into staying asleep for so long. I am furious when I think of so many friends who have also fallen asleep while Satan wreaks havoc on their homes. How angry do you get when you realize the enemy has been manipulating you all this time with his lies and his evil schemes? It should infuriate you, too.

But can I tell you what enrages Satan more than anything? It is when you finally "Get *UP!*" When you understand that you are a child of God and the power of the Holy Spirit lives inside of you to accomplish all of God's agenda on this earth, the enemy trembles. He is more afraid of you than you should be of him because he knows what you are capable of doing in your community, state, and country. Just imagine if we filled our nations with godly leaders who have a fear of the Lord. When believers rise up, the whole world can be transformed as each of us carries God's heart into all the earth. Once you realize your identity in Christ, you become a threat to the devil's agenda, and he knows he is powerless to mess with you anymore. All his schemes and agenda go out the door the moment you wake up.

WHO IS YOUR WAKE-UP CALL?

Remember that first women's conference in Australia? While on the plane, I heard God speak to me through my friend Lisa Bevere's book, *Out of Control and Loving It*. As I read through the pages of this book, my eyes were opened wide, and I was able to hear God's voice with clarity and see what He was doing in my life. God was at this conference, and I was one of thousands who heard the call to rise up and be alert! I was challenged to avoid hitting the snooze button, so I would not fall back to sleep.

Ephesians 5:14 (NLT) says:

"Awake, O Sleeper, rise up from the dead,
and Christ will give you light."

You and I may not be physically dead like Lazarus, but we might be lifeless on the inside and need revival or simply a slap across the face—figuratively speaking—to wake up. Sometimes as people are trying to wake up after a deep sleep, they slap their cheeks to get their blood circulating. A spiritual slap or shake of the shoulder is often what people need to get them up and moving. Can you tell my love language is physical touch? I do not have any problem giving you a slap if that is what is needed to wake you up. Just kidding, I promise . . . but if you really need a slap, just let me know.

Over the years, we have all been slapped by the Word of God as we engage in our devotions, listen to a podcast, lean into the pastor's message, or respond to the counsel of a godly friend. God will use anything and everything to wake you up, so you are able to hear His words for your life. You just need to wake up.

Don't you want friends who are willing to spiritually slap you by speaking truth into your life when you need it most? I want to be that kind of friend. Once you get to know me, you will realize that I do not like to pretend or be fake. I don't sugarcoat what I need to say. I prefer to shoot straight and be direct, provided I am tactful and use the right tone. Don't we have enough people in this world saying the things we want to hear? How about a friend who actually cares enough to tell you the truth even if it may offend you or cause some discomfort? As Proverbs 27:6 (NLT) says:

"Wounds from a sincere friend are better
than many kisses from an enemy."

At the end of the day, wouldn't we rather hear the truth than live a lie? I have friends who are willing to give me a wake-up call when I need one.

I remember one friend who brought to my attention my leadership style, sharing that my team felt all I did was tell them what to do rather than ask for assistance. Did this hurt my feelings? Of course, but I had to suck it up because I knew there was also a lot of accuracy to what she said. In order for me to change, I had to receive the truth about my leadership. I had to learn how to be the kind of leader who welcomes the team to bring ideas to the table rather than merely dictating what I wanted.

What about you? Do you have friends who are trying to speak truth into your life or figuratively slap your cheeks to wake you up from your sleep? Have you been listening? It is time we wake up and become open to the truth because only then can God bring change into our marriages, homes, parenting, and relationships. At the end of the day, whom do you have in your circle of friends who is willing to give you that wake-up call when necessary? Are you the kind of friend who doesn't mind stepping on toes to wake someone up from their snooze?

WHAT DOES IT LOOK LIKE WHEN YOU'RE WIDE AWAKE?

What is it like when you are up and wide awake? Let's revisit the story of Lazarus in John 11. Once the stone was rolled from the tomb, Jesus commanded Lazarus to "come out" and Lazarus got up! Can you imagine the reactions of the people surrounding the grave? Here was a man who was quite dead but was now very much miraculously alive.

What a tremendous loss it would have been to the community if Lazarus had remained permanently asleep. I bet you that, after he got up, Lazarus moved forward with such renewed passion and strength that he was empowered to accomplish more than he had ever done for his community. Keep in mind that Lazarus had been in the tomb for four days. When a Jewish person died, the custom was to tightly wrap the feet together and hands to the side of the body with linen. The deceased person's face was covered with a cloth. When Jesus called forth Lazarus from his sleep,

> *"the dead man came out, his hands and feet wrapped with strips of linen and a cloth around his face" (v. 44).*

What was the first thing that Jesus told the witnesses when Lazarus woke up from the dead? Jesus said to them, "Take off the grave clothes and let him go."

When you are wide awake, you are just like a dead person who suddenly has come back to life. The things that once held you in bondage, whether fear, complacency, shame, or guilt, fall to the wayside as you walk forward to embrace the plans God has for your life. No longer covered by a cloth, your eyes are wide open and ready to see all that God is doing in the world and plans to do through you. You are ready to let go of the lies the enemy has tried to bury you with and exchange it for garments of truth.

When I returned from the women's conference, I felt like I was Lazarus waking up from a long sleep. I returned with greater passion, deeper vision, and renewed enthusiasm for the future. I felt an urgency to get everything done yesterday. I longed for women to hear and see what God was doing in the state of Hawai'i. I needed to convey the message that women must get up and open their eyes to see their potential for making an impact right here, right now. That is what it looks like when a child of God is wide awake. A fully awake person takes every opportunity to make a difference and make life count.

God is still in the business of bringing things back to life. I have witnessed marriages restored when a fully awake person chooses to forgive an unfaithful spouse. I have witnessed a person be completely healed of cancer when the doctor has given them only months to live all because people woke up to their calling and began to pray without ceasing. When God resurrects us from sleep, we should come back to life more grateful, with a renewed sense of purpose to do everything God wants us to do while here on earth.

I remember walking alongside a friend during a difficult season in her marriage after her husband admitted to being unfaithful while deployed. Although it rocked her world, and she found herself with little direction, she and her husband made the decision to get up together. With a repentant heart, her husband chose to fight for their marriage as they both attended Celebrate Recovery, a ministry for anyone struggling with hurt, pain, or addiction. Although it was tempting for this couple to hit the snooze button and fall back to sleep, they remained fully awake and committed to staying together. It was challenging, but this husband and wife kept their eyes wide open, attending a connect group of fellow believers for a solid year and witnessing God slowly bring healing to their marriage. My friend describes this season as a wake-up call as neither had realized how much their marriage needed to be resuscitated. Today, my friend and her husband are happier than the day they were married, all because they both woke up and discovered what they have with one another.

There is an urgency as I am writing this book. In John 9:4-5 (NLT), it says:

"We must quickly carry out the tasks assigned to us by the one who sent us. The night is coming

and then no one can work. But while I'm here
in the world, I am the light of the world."

No one knows the day or time when Jesus will return. If 2020 has taught us anything, it is that we are not guaranteed tomorrow. While there is still time, we must realize what is at stake. We are called to wake up and be about God's business. It is time to throw off the grave clothes of mediocrity and pursue a life filled with intentionality and purpose. God has assigned each of us a task. Together, as we rise up, let us be an army that continues to tell others, *"**Hey, Wake UP!**"* Then, listen, as you hear the enemy cry out in terrified shrieks, "Oh Crap, She's UP!" However, waking up means much more than just opening your eyes. What happens next when you decide to permanently turn off that snooze button and throw off the covers of the enemy? Well, keep reading because there is so much more!

02.

SHE REALIZES WHO SHE IS

But one thing I do know, that though
I was blind, now I see.
—John 9:25

Most people sleep with their eyes closed. When we allow the enemy to convince us that we need to hit the snooze button, our eyes remain closed, and we become oblivious to what is going on around us. The good news is that God has the power to release us from this blindness, whether we are physically or spiritually blind. In John 9, Jesus healed a beggar who had been blind since birth. The disciples assumed that his blindness was the result of either his sinfulness or that of his parents, a somewhat common belief that diseases were the direct result of God's judgment on sin. Jesus explained that the man's blindness was not the result of sin but happened so that the works of God might be displayed through him.

Jesus spit on the ground and put mud made from saliva on the man's eyes, telling him to wash in the Pool of Siloam. The man obeyed Jesus and came home seeing. Like this man who was physically blind, we can become spiritually blind to the truth. What then can set us free from our blindness? Truth can only be revealed through the power of the Holy Spirit and the Word of God. When God reveals the truth about you or about a situation, you can experience freedom like never before. What are the truths that the Holy Spirit needs to reveal in your life to set you free so that you wake up and stop snoozing? We all say we want the truth, but some of us only want to hear partial truth. We find it difficult to handle the whole truth and nothing but the truth. What is it that causes us to stop short of embracing the truth revealed to us by the Holy Spirit? Perhaps we are holding on to pride, fear, or complacency, causing the truth to be distorted and our vision clouded.

When Mike and I were first married, I struggled to love my stepdaughter because of her constant rejection of me. The hurt was deep, so Mike and I chose to begin counseling. Although the counselor encouraged me to show love to my stepdaughter, her rejection of me time and time again made it difficult. One day my mom confronted me. "You are supposed to be a Christian and love your stepdaughter as if she is your own daughter." The words were tough to swallow not only because I knew it was the truth, but my mom was not a Christian, and my actions were not a good reflection of Jesus in my life. The truth of the matter is that I was not living like a Christian because I should have been loving my stepdaughter unconditionally, whether or not she accepted or rejected my love. My anger, frustration, and hurt had prevented me from waking up, opening my eyes to the truth, and loving my stepdaughter through my words and actions.

When a child of God wakes up, suddenly everything around them springs to life, and they realize what they have been missing. Realization is the act of becoming fully aware of something as a fact with understanding or comprehension of what has become the reality. Have you ever attempted to solve a math problem to no avail? You work the problem over and over, but no matter how many times you try, you arrive at the wrong answer. Suddenly, you remember something you were taught in class and everything clicks together. You not only get the right answer, but you also now understand how to solve the problem. The moment of this discovery, you let out a resounding, "YES!" in celebration of your accomplishment.

Realization can also be compared to instantly hitting the jackpot or finally comprehending the complex meaning behind an artist's masterpiece. It is an epiphany moment. That is exactly what happens when you open your eyes and realize the truth of who you are and to whom you belong. The truth sets you free as God's Word clicks in your brain and makes sense at last.

God has been telling us and showing us since Old Testament days who we are. Just look at David who was anointed king over Israel although he was the youngest of his brothers and tended sheep for a living. Gideon was referred to as a mighty man of valor even though he was beating wheat in the winepress to hide from the Midianites. 1 Samuel 16:7 stresses that the Lord does not see as man sees. The world looks at our outward appearance, such as height or stature, but God looks at our heart. Unfortunately, we have allowed the enemy to cloud our vision. Instead of embracing God's truth, we have become confused along the journey of life, empowering the enemy to define our identity. It is easy to become distracted by competing voices telling us who we are and who we are supposed to be. We do not have to look far to realize that social media, advertising, and the media often portray an image of who we should be that is quite contrary to the Word of God.

I have three daughters, each with different personalities and gifts that make them unique. From the time they were young, Mike and I were determined to be the strongest voices in their lives because we knew they would have many people speaking over them, some positive but many negative. We knew the most confusing season for them would be during their teen years, just as they began to like boys.

Although I tried my best to convince my girls that "boys are bad," my attempts at manipulation did not work. I knew I could control their time on the phone and limit which friends they were allowed to go out with on weekends, but the one thing I could not control was their hearts. As much as I wanted to protect my girls from heartache, whom they would fall in love with was a matter of the heart and well beyond my control. When I came to the truth of this realization, I had to completely trust God and keep my eyes focused on Him. Mike and I continued to tell our daughters not to give their hearts away, reminding them that their father was the first one to say, "You are beautiful, and I love you."

While we wanted to shield our girls from boys who would try to manipulate and deceive them with their words, we recognized it would be difficult to protect them from heartache when they fell in love. Nevertheless, we are committed to be the voice that speaks life into our girls, helping them navigate their hearts with wisdom and discernment when it comes to relationships. Like my daughters, we too, must learn to guard our hearts and minds, so we are fully awake and able to discern between the competing voices that either tell us the truth or a lie.

How can we distinguish the truth from lies? You will always know the truth when you measure the voices against the Word of God and ask the Holy Spirit to open your eyes and speak to your heart.

"But when He, the Spirit of truth, comes, He will guide you into all the truth. He will not speak on His own; He will speak only what He hears, and He will tell you what is yet to come" (John 16:13, NIV).

Sheep are not the smartest animals of God's creation, but they tune into the voice of their shepherd. They have come to know his voice and trust the shepherd for protection and guidance. It is said that sheep will run in fear from unfamiliar voices or those they don't understand. John 10:27 (NIV) paints a beautiful picture of how the sheep listen to the voice of the shepherd:

"I know them, and they follow Me."

How can you know the voice of God? You must spend time getting to know Him. God knows us very well, but do we know Him? For me, I hear God's voice as I read His Word during daily devotions or during my walks on the beach. I have been going on "dates" with Jesus on the beach now for over three years. When I realized that I needed to set aside time to be alone with Jesus, I began calendaring these "dates" into my schedule each week.

Imagine for a moment that you plan a date with someone you love, only to get caught up in the busyness of the day, causing you to skip or cancel. Week after week, something more important comes up, and you have to "reschedule" your date. It would not be long before you began growing apart from the one you love. How can you know someone intimately if you are not willing to carve out precious time to spend with them? The more time I spend with Jesus, the more I can hear God speaking through word pictures He gives me.

God communicates in different ways to different people. It might be through a song, a word picture, a prophetic word, a verse in the Bible, or nature. Do not make the mistake of boxing God in and thinking He only speaks one way. The key here is that you make time to spend alone with God so that you can know Him like sheep to the shepherd. I had to learn how to discern His voice over the many competing voices surrounding me, including my own. Only when I woke up and opened my eyes was I able to understand the truth of who I am. That realization of the truth empowered me to ignore every other deceptive voice and listen only to the voice of Jesus. What freedom a woman experiences when she realizes who she is in Christ!

What happens when you realize you have been manipulated or deceived? Perhaps you get angry or feel embarrassed that you allowed yourself to be hoodwinked. Have you ever bought that "magic facial cream" because it was guaranteed to turn back the hands of time and make you look ten years younger? The seller was so convincing, but you quickly became disillusioned when it failed to measure up. The promises of youth were attempts at deception ... and they worked. I absolutely hate being manipulated or deceived in any way and do not appreciate anyone who operates in manipulation or deception. These people are consumed with getting what they want without regard to how many get hurt or are deceived in the process. Do you know anyone like this? I have been deceived by people who I thought wanted my friendship.

Years ago, when God led me to establish our annual Arise Women's Conference at Inspire Church, the Holy Spirit told me to protect the platform from deceptive and manipulative people. I have encountered people in the past decade who I thought wanted my friendship, later to realize they were hoping to use the Arise platform to push their agenda. If they were unsuccessful with me, they tried to manipulate my husband. Thankfully, we are both protectors by nature, so we constantly pray that God gives us discernment, so we can know the truth from lies.

God has given us a responsibility to make certain that we only carry out His agenda on the platform with which

He has entrusted us. No matter what you do in life, there will always be people who manipulate or try to deceive you to get what they want. Therefore, you must be fully awake and in tune with the voice of the Holy Spirit. When we come to the realization that we are being manipulated or deceived, it is important that we no longer welcome those people into our circle of friends. Friends who deceive and manipulate are not your friends. Leviticus 25:17 (NIV) expresses this another way:

> *"Do not take advantage of each other, but fear your God. I am the Lord your God."*

When you get up and open your eyes, you will be able to surround yourself with friends who build you up and help you to fulfill the vision God has for your life. Have you ever wondered why people feel the need to manipulate or deceive? I believe manipulation is borne out of a need to control the outcome by taking advantage of innocent people. People deceive and manipulate in order to get what they want. Romans 16:18 (NIV) describes them this way:

"For such people are not serving our Lord Christ,
but their own appetites. By smooth talk and flattery
they deceive the minds of naïve people."

There are countless men and women in the Bible who manipulated and deceived to get what they wanted. In Genesis 27, Rebecca deceived her husband, Isaac, because she wanted the blessing to go to her younger son, Jacob, rather than her older son, Esau, as would be tradition. So great was her manipulation that she urged her son to impersonate his brother by dressing in Esau's clothes and covering his arms and hands in goatskins. When Jacob brought his father his favorite meal prepared by Rebecca, Isaac was deceived into blessing him because his eyes were weak, and he could no longer see. What an elaborate scheme just to ensure that the blessing went to the younger son whom Rebecca loved the most.

Remember Abram (later given the name Abraham by God), the great man of faith in the Old Testament whom God called the Father of Many Nations? Did you know that even Abram was guilty of deception? In Exodus 10:10-20, Abram was afraid that Pharaoh would kill him when he saw Abram's beautiful wife Sarai (later called

Sarah by God). Because he wanted to live, Abram convinced Sarai to lie and say she was his sister. Pharoah took Sarai into his palace, but God intervened and caused terrible plagues on Pharaoh's household until he let Abram and Sarai go.

Despite their manipulation and deceit, the outcomes of these men and women did not go as planned. Have deception and manipulation caused you to end up with nothing or less than what you expected as you sought to control an outcome that you desperately wanted? To be completely honest, I have been guilty of manipulation many times in my life—both as a child and an adult—to get my way. Why? Although I have never tried to take advantage of innocent people, like Rebecca and Abram, I have attempted to control an outcome to achieve my purposes. (How do you think I got Mike? I'm joking!) When I woke up and drew closer to the Lord, I came to this realization about myself and had to repent. I learned that I needed to trust God for His outcomes rather than mine. Because I had turned off snooze and my eyes were wide open, God revealed an aspect of me that was not easy to swallow, but I knew this truth would ultimately set me free. It enabled me to allow God to change me.

Once I released control, I was able to trust God with all my outcomes, placing God's will above my own—serving Him rather than my own self-interests.

From the time I was a child, I was deceived and manipulated into believing I would never be enough—not smart enough, pretty enough, or good enough. Maybe it was the way I was raised or the messages I received from watching television and following social media. Whether it was an advertisement for the latest trend or a comparison between myself and other women who appeared to have it all together on Instagram or Facebook, I would hear that familiar voice in my head that told me I would never measure up.

Satan is the master manipulator. He knows when God's children are snoozing and takes advantage by reminding us over and over again of the lies that we have believed about ourselves. It is time to GET UP and listen to God's voice. It is time to realize that you are more than enough! You are qualified, accepted, appreciated, loved, and good because God said you are.

When I gave my life to Jesus many years ago, one of my first prayers was for wisdom and discernment because I needed to know what was right and wrong. I knew I had to practice listening to the Holy Spirit, so I could distinguish truth from the lies. Hebrews 5:14 (NIV) puts it this way:

> *"But solid food is for the mature, who by constant use have trained themselves to distinguish good from evil."*

I needed to train myself. God began to open my eyes to the truths that eventually set me free, but it took time and patience to wean me from the lies of the enemy that I had believed for so long. Over the past ten years or so, I have come to realize just how much Satan had been deceiving me and manipulating me with his lies. I had forgotten who I am in Christ. It is high time to GET UP and get angry at Satan. He has been manipulating us far too long. With eyes wide open and a newfound realization of truth, it is time to do something about it.

01. Don't just sit there and let the master of deception keep manipulating you. His ultimate goal is to keep you asleep so that you do not awaken and realize who you are and what you're capable of doing for the Kingdom of God. GET UP!

02. Realizing your identity in Jesus Christ will set your new foundation on a solid rock that cannot be shaken or moved. Romans 10:9 (ESV) says, "If you confess with your mouth that Jesus is Lord and believe in your heart that God raised Him from the dead, you will be saved." When we do this, God acknowledges us as His sons and daughters, and He stamps us as His own. BELIEVE!

03. We have belonging, a place, a seat at the table, a position and worth that are greater than the value of diamonds. Satan knows this, and that is why when you are up, your understanding and realization of whose you are starts to make sense. This is the most important step in the realization of your identity in Christ because this sets the course for your future and everything that you will be doing will make sense. You will understand what you are made of and how to operate your skills for God's plans and not your own plans. YOU HAVE A SEAT!

The realization of who you are is paramount to your future. Satan has been blinding you too long, keeping you from seeing who you really are. He is delighted each time you hit the snooze button rather than fully waking up. The deception is real, and his manipulation has caused you to become tangled in a web of lies. Allow God to untangle the web, and allow His truth to wean you off the lies. It is time to wake up and embrace your true identity in Christ.

03.

SHE GETS THINGS DONE!

Now that you have opened your eyes and are beginning to realize who you are in Christ and that you belong to the King of Kings, what comes next? A child of God who GETS UP is able to Get Things Done!

Acts 9:36-43 (NIV) portrays the beautiful story of a woman named Tabitha (also called Dorcas in Greek) who was "always doing good and helping the poor." What a legacy! With just a few simple but powerful words, this Bible passage sums up her life. Tabitha was a woman who refused to hit the snooze button and let the enemy deceive her into remaining oblivious to the world around her. She was always—not sometimes ... or only when she felt like it ... but always—doing good. Tabitha knew who she was and used her talent of sewing to meet the needs of those around her, whether clothing the widows or giving part of her earnings to bless the poor in the city of Joppa. I would love to have met Tabitha, just to have the opportunity to talk with her. What a selfless woman she must have been, using her gifts to help those in need. The loss of her life would have been a loss to the community. Tabitha had a purpose to fulfill, and she had no intention of letting the enemy lull her to sleep. Fully awake with eyes wide open, she lived out that purpose and, as a result, got things done.

Sadly, Tabitha became sick one day and eventually died, causing the widows to tearfully reminisce about the robes and other clothing she had made for them while still alive. At the insistence of the disciples, Peter went to see Tabitha. When he arrived at her upstairs room, Peter got on his knees to pray and commanded Tabitha to get up! She opened her eyes and sat up. Peter helped her to her feet so that she was presented to the believers, especially the widows, very much alive. I can only imagine how much more Tabitha must have done for her community once she realized that one day, she would not be here on earth to do good.

Some of us are still spiritually asleep. Like Tabitha and Lazarus, we must get up and get on our feet if we are to fulfill the purposes God has for our lives. If you were given a second chance in life, how would you serve your community? Would you do something different? Would you strive to always do good? God calls us to get things done while we still have breath and strength.

I am not sure if you are like me, but I like checklists. I cannot go to the grocery store without making a checklist, and I must have a calendar that reminds me what I have to do today, throughout the week, and the coming month at a glance. I need to be able to check things off my list, so I know I completed my tasks for the day. This type of person is often called a control freak! Well, I am a proud control freak. Do you know why? I get things done! I set goals, and my checklists and calendar help me know I have accomplished something meaningful for myself or someone else.

Are we making the same types of checklists when it comes to things God is asking us to accomplish? Are you getting things done for Jesus? What are you doing with the gifts God has given you? Are you using them to always do good and serve others in your family, neighborhood, church, community, city, state, or country? There will come a day when you meet Jesus face to face, and He will ask you this very question.

> *"And all were judged according to their deeds (works)," (Revelation 20:13, NLT).*

Will you, like Tabitha, be able to say that you always did good with what God has given you?

I am adamant about using the gifts God has so graciously given each of us *today* as we work and serve others *while* we are here on earth—not tomorrow, next week, or next month but today. In 2 Timothy 1:6 (NIV), Paul encouraged Timothy to "fan into flame the gift of God."

If a campfire is left unattended long enough, it begins to smolder or dwindle down to embers until you blow fresh oxygen over them to fan the flames. This introduction of fresh air causes the fire to reignite, producing warmth that radiates throughout the campsite.

When we neglect the gifts that God has given us, it is as if we are leaving our fires unattended until they eventually burn out and are no longer useful. We forget that God has equipped us with all the gifts necessary to fulfill His unique purpose for our lives. Only when we allow the

Holy Spirit to breathe a fresh wind over our gifts and fan the flames are we able to meet the needs of those around us. Perhaps we have allowed the enemy to blind us, so we only see the gifts in others, but not ourselves. 1 Timothy 4:14 (NLT) urges us to "not neglect the spiritual gift you received through the prophecy spoken over you when the elders of the church laid their hands on you."

Maybe you are unaware of the gifts God has equipped you with to get things done. 1 Peter 4:10 (NIV) urges,

> *"Each of you should use whatever gift you have*
> *received to serve others, as faithful stewards*
> *of God's grace in its various forms."*

What are these spiritual gifts, and how can we determine the gifts God has placed in our lives? 1 Corinthians 12:7-11 mentions some of these gifts as wisdom, knowledge, faith, healing, miracles, prophecy, discernment, tongues, and interpretation of tongues. In Romans 12:6-8, we learn that other spiritual gifts include prophecy, service, teaching, encouragement, giving, leadership, and mercy. Other gifts in action mentioned in 1 Corinthians 12:28 include apostles, prophets, teachers, miracle workers, healers, helpers, and those who guide and speak in tongues.

What we must remember is that each of us has gifts unique to us.

> *There are different kinds of gifts, but the same Spirit distributes them. There are different kinds of service, but the same Lord. There are different kinds of working, but in all of them and in everyone it is the same God at work.* —*1 Corinthians 12:4-6 (NIV)*

When identifying your spiritual gifts, it is important to surround yourself with believers who can see what you cannot see and are able to point out gifts that are evident in your life. If we are going to get things done for God, we must be willing to not only call out the gifts we see in one another but also inspire others to operate in those gifts. We must spend time with God, reading His Word and asking Him to reveal and make clear the gifts He has given us. I would also encourage you to sign up for a class like Inspire Church's Growth Track that encourages you to discover your gifts and fan them into flame.

When you are up, you will be like Tabitha and get things done. You will not be wasting time because you understand that time is precious. You will know who you are because you are fully awake to what God is doing here on earth. You will no longer be content to remain complacent or hit the snooze button during your watch. If we are to use our gifts to get things done, we must guard against wasting our time on meaningless activities that distract us from our calling and assignment. What are some of these meaningless things that steal away our time? One of the biggest weapons the enemy uses to distract us from getting things done is our relationships—the ones that will not take us to where we need to be. There are two types of relationships that can become stumbling blocks to our getting up and getting things done: courtships and friendships.

COURTSHIP OR "MORE THAN A FRIEND" GROUP

Is it possible that you are dating someone not aligned to your future? I am talking about a relationship that adds no weight to your destiny and is actually draining your emotions and occupying your time with things that will never make a difference. Was that too straight up? I am only trying to help you.

How do you know if you are dating someone who is a distraction? Eventually you will begin to notice he is doing his own thing and leaving you out. You will find yourself complaining, "I just wish he would lead us spiritually instead of me always having to pray and share my devotions." The Bible is clear that we should not be teaming up with unbelievers (2 Corinthians 6:14). Well, what if the person you are dating is a Christian and a really nice guy? At the end of the day, is this someone who is going to lead you to what God is calling the both of you to do? Or is he wasting your time and forcing you to put your calling on the shelf, so he can do what he wants to do, and you are just along for the ride? I am not saying it is wrong to follow someone you love, but you must ensure the person is leading you in God's direction for your life.

If you are not married and are already questioning this "nice guy" or complaining about his lack of spiritual guidance, you have an opportunity to make a U-turn and adjust the path that you are on right now. I could go on and on about this, but you get my heart. I promise you;

you will thank me later when you are married to the one God has chosen for you—the person who encourages you to use your gifts to get things done. I am being optimistic for your sake—get out of the relationship now!

What if you are married, and your spouse is not aligned to God's purposes for your life? Let me encourage you to keep your vows and ask God to work on your heart. Pray that God will help you learn to be content but never complacent in your marriage. Find ways to work together, and ask God to help you encourage your spouse so that he operates in his gifts and grows in his walk with the Lord. You are a team, and you must stick together as a team. Do not allow the enemy to distract you into engaging in things that ultimately tear you and your marriage apart. Find a ministry where you both can serve together and use your gifts to further God's Kingdom as husband and wife.

FRIENDSHIPS

We all need friends, but which circle of friends encourages and helps you get to where God is calling you? I have learned over the years that all of the friends in our friendship circles matter. You may have a circle of friends with whom you hang out when you want to have fun and another circle that supports you as you build your family. But do you have a circle of friends that challenges you to new heights and helps you expand your vision? These friends may not necessarily be older but are ahead of you in their calling or careers. These friends are role models because they are getting things done by operating in God's calling and using their gifts to make a difference. We need all of these friendship circles because they each play an important role as we journey through life.

What happens when you are stuck with friends who continually disappoint or criticize you or remain complacent with life because they continue with old habits and refuse to change? These are people who do not understand you are growing in your faith and want to believe there is more to life than what this friend group has to offer. While I realize I can have many friends, my closest circle is made up of those friends who inspire and encourage me to live out my best life as a woman, wife, mother, and friend. I want to surround myself with friends who help me see things I have never seen before—people who will be an influence on my future and cheer for me as I reach my full potential in Christ.

Develop the kinds of friends who help you to be "perfectly you." Sound familiar? Sadly, people are so committed to their friendships that they sacrifice their calling, potential, and gifts just so they can remain in those friendship circles. If your friends are not adding to your life but only taking from you, perhaps it is time you reevaluate those relationships.

There is one final group that I consider meaningless because it takes away time from your getting things done—your *social media* or *fan group*. You follow a person or group, and suddenly you feel like you have a new friend when in reality, you are just part of their fan group. They want you to like them and become a fan not because they want to be your friend but simply so they can gain more popularity.

I am not knocking social media. I have joined several social media sites and believe in their purpose to connect people from across the globe. The problem is that social media can become a huge distraction to getting up and getting things done when all you see is what the world wants you to see. You jump online and see the great things people are doing, the fabulous clothes they are wearing, and the timeless products they are promoting to turn back the hands of time. You allow the enemy to deceive you into believing that you must act or look a certain way to be successful. You forget your identity in Christ and become suckered into buying beauty products that promise to enhance your looks but fail to deliver.

I get it! Nice shoes, great jackets, ageless beauty products, the latest entertainment gossip—all the while we are being lured back into sleep as we waste hours upon hours on social media when we should be getting things done! When will you get tired of all this?

I believe we have become so unhappy with how we look and what we have because we continue comparing ourselves to those perfectly happy people on social media. We, once again, close our eyes to the truth and see only what people want us to see. How many people actually share their struggles on social media or post pictures that are unfiltered and possibly unflattering? Not many! Most of the posts on social media show the good times, celebrations, or major milestones. Media can drive you to the point of stress, anxiety, frustration, and unhappiness as you compare your life with those who appear to look better, seem to have more, or act as if they feel happier. I get that we can find amazing information on social media, read encouraging stories, and discover data that we need, but let us not become so distracted that we forget who we are in Christ. It is okay to be a fan, but remember that your fan friend is different from your inner circle of friends who will be there for you in good and bad times.

When you are up and wide awake, you will realize that relationships and friendships can either move you toward God's purposes for your life or hinder your potential, keeping you from getting things done. Like Tabitha, you were designed with a specific purpose that only you can do. You were created to accomplish a whole lot more than you realize and equipped with gifts unique to you. Would you believe me if I told you that the greatest potential lies within you because you are destined to do mighty and amazing things for the Kingdom?

When she gets UP, she gets things done! Knowing that you are empowered to get things done, how will you strategize your day, week, or even your life? What will your checklist look like? If you made a list of everything God is calling you to do, you probably would not be able to accomplish everything in your lifetime. There would be no talk of retirement because you would have too much to do and not enough time to get it all done. My desire is that you live out your full potential in Christ so that you can look back on your life and say, "Wow, I am so glad I took myself out of that relationship, friendship, or mindset that said I have to be like everyone else instead of being perfectly me."

My friend, let me encourage you to get up, open your eyes, and like Tabitha, get things done that only you can do. Get going and stay awake because you have too much that God wants you to do in this lifetime. Stay awake, and resist the temptation to hit the snooze button, causing you to fall back into the same old patterns of engaging in meaningless activities that distract you from your potential. Fill your days with relationships and friendships that push you forward—not backward into old habits. I cannot wait to see how you are getting things done and how God uses your gifts when you are up and wide awake.

04.

SHE IS FOCUSED AND FIERCE

God calls all Christians to be watchmen, but what exactly does that mean? The word watchman comes from the Hebrew verb meaning "to look out or about, spy or keep watch, lean forward, observe and await." In biblical times, watchmen stood guard in watchtowers or on city walls to protect the community from thieves, animals, or an approaching enemy. The watchman was the first line of defense against any approaching threat. You would never catch the watchman snoozing!

In Ezekiel 3:16-21, the prophet Ezekiel is commissioned or appointed to serve as a watchman over Israel. In this role, Ezekiel was responsible for warning the rebellious people to turn from their evil ways while encouraging the righteous to keep from sinning in order to save their lives. Jesus told his disciples in Mark 14:38 (NIV):

"Watch and pray so you will not fall into temptation."

Jesus understood the importance of being a watchman and standing guard against attacks from the enemy as he explained to his disciples that "the spirit is willing, but the flesh is weak."

Did the watchman ever get too comfortable perched on the tower and drift off to sleep? What would be the harm if he closed his eyes for just a few minutes? Isaiah 62:6 (ESV) illustrates how watchmen are required to stay alert at all times:

"On your walls, oh Jerusalem, I have set watchmen.
All the day and all the night, they shall never be
silent. You who put the Lord in remembrance, take
no rest, and give him no rest until he establishes
Jerusalem and makes it a praise in the earth."

For the watchman, there was no time for snoozing. He needed to be on guard, looking ahead 24/7, and waiting with expectation until the day God fulfilled His promises. Fully awake, the watchman was fierce and focused—continuing to watch, continuing to pray, and continuing to believe all day and all night. What is God asking you to keep watch over or observe?

Since I was called to pastor Inspire with Mike twenty years ago, I have felt God leading me to be a watchman over the church. I remember praying in those early days that God would equip us to shepherd the people He would bring to Inspire. I believed God would bring people from all walks of life but particularly those with similar backgrounds to ours—single parents, divorced, blended families, and people struggling with their identity in Christ. We not only love every person who walks through the doors of Inspire Church, we care for the people in surrounding communities outside the church. Everywhere you turn, people are hurting as they struggle to overcome physical, financial, and emotional challenges. I believe the church is the answer to every problem. Like Ezekiel and the disciples, God is commissioning us to be watchmen over the earth, and we all have a part to play beginning with our families and communities.

Within the span of two years, we witnessed our entire world change. We can all agree that since 2020, our country is no longer the same. Many Christians who survived the Spanish Flu and AIDS that claimed the lives of millions are now faced with confronting yet another global pandemic. For younger generations, COVID-19 is a virus like none other, taking the lives of over 750,000 in the US alone. The testimonies of those who overcame the battles of previous pandemics give us hope for today—that someday, there will be another chapter to this painful time in history when we look back and speak of our resilience.

As a watchman for over twenty years, I can say with certainty that I have never seen God more alive than now as He continues to work all things out for our good. I believe God is working through His people, stirring them to wake up from their slumber and focus with a fierceness on what the enemy is doing in our families, community, Hawai'i, our nation, and the world. It is time for God's children to focus their gaze as watchmen and recognize that the enemy is using the pandemic to create division, tension, and hostility toward one another.

Unfortunately, I believe Christians have fallen asleep on their watch. With all that is going on in the world today, God needs for every believer to rise up and become a watchman for Jesus.

Being a watchman requires that believers be dressed and ready for service at all times. Whatever God calls you to watch over, you must do so wholeheartedly and with expectation. A watchman must be focused and prepared, just like five of the bridesmaids in Matthew 25. Jesus told a story of ten virgins who were waiting for the arrival of a bridegroom. It was Jewish custom for the bride to wait at home for the groom with her closest friends until he arrived sometime in the evening and escorted her to her new home. The only problem was that no one but the groom's father knew when the groom would arrive.

When the groom arrived to take his bride, the bridesmaids would light the streets with their lamps in a procession toward the wedding feast. Unlike lamps of today, these required oil in order to burn and produce light. Five of the virgins were considered "foolish" because they failed to bring oil with them. Perhaps they were snoozing and forgot the oil or refused to focus and were deceived by the enemy into believing they did not need to bring oil.

The remaining five virgins were called "wise" because they were prepared. They took oil in jars along with their lamps so that as they watched and waited with expectation, their lamps continuously burned no matter how long it took for the bridegroom to arrive.

At midnight when the bridegroom arrived, the five virgins trimmed their lamps and were able to celebrate with the bridegroom. On the other hand, the five foolish virgins were forced to leave the home and buy oil, returning only to find that the bridegroom had left for the wedding banquet with the wise virgins, shutting the door behind them. Are you keeping watch with your lamp burning, prepared to immediately open the door for the master whenever He knocks?

Are you up and dressed for service like the wise virgins? Do you have enough oil for your journey? When you are wide awake, you will need sufficient oil to enable you to focus on the tasks God has called you to accomplish with fierceness.

Have you ever met a woman so focused on the task at hand that nothing and no one could distract her from getting things done? Sounds a lot like me when I start cleaning the house. I am determined to get it all done before I go on to the next thing. My family knows that when I come back from a vacation or a business trip, I have to unpack all my clothes, put them in the wash, place all things where they belong—including the luggage—and clean the kitchen counter and floors. My husband and children know it is impossible to stop me from this routine because I have been doing the same thing for over twenty-five years. Nothing has changed.

My family has also discovered it is best to stay out of my way during this time because if they try to distract me, I will ask them to clean along with me. It could be to clean their rooms or rearrange the entire garage. When I am focused, my children know not to ask Mom if she can make lunch. Duh! Granted, my children are all at the age they can prepare a meal themselves.

Have you ever noticed the eyes of a woman who is focused on getting her tasks done? Her eyes are fierce, almost scary, as if she is Superwoman who has the power to cut through a diamond or pierce your heart with her fiery eyes. This is a picture of a woman who is focused and fierce. As she watches from her tower, she is awake and aware of everything happening around her. She is aware of the calling on her life and keeps oil in her lamp so that nothing goes unnoticed because she is focused on the spiritual atmosphere.

When a woman of God gets up, her discernment is high because she refuses to allow distractions to keep her from getting things done. That, my friend, is what it will be like when you are fully awake. What we need is for more of you to become focused and fierce, ready to take aim and fire back at the schemes of the enemy. You and I need to wake up and look out as watchmen and watchwomen. With renewed focus, we need to see how the enemy is gaining ground through our system of government, affecting our freedom of choice and greatly impacting our children and grandchildren for generations to come.

The enemy was trying to divide marriages, split up families and destroy communities, well before the pandemic. We can no longer allow the enemy to take any more ground. It is time to wake up and draw the line against the enemy's attack on justice and freedom. Remember, Satan is afraid of you because he is aware how laser-focused you can be when you become determined to finally wake up and stand your ground as a watchman.

There were many women in the Bible who were focused and fierce. I like to call them warriors for Christ.

One of the fiercest women who comes to mind is Deborah, who led the Israelite army to victory in a battle against the Canaanites and their commander, Sisera, in Judges 4-5. Both a judge and prophetess, Deborah told Barak to take ten thousand men of Naphtali and Zebulun and lead them up to Mount Tabor. Barak was willing to go, but only if Deborah accompanied him. She must have been a fierce woman of God with laser-focused eyes. In Judges 5, Deborah recognized that Israel refused to fight because of fear until she made the decision to rise up as a mother in Israel (v 7). She understood the calling on her life and was willing to get up to ensure that she accomplished her God-given task.

Under the command of Barak, ten thousand men journeyed to Mount Tabor along with Deborah, causing Sisera to abandon his chariot and flee on foot into the tent of Jael, wife of a Kenite. Jael was another fierce woman who continued to keep her lamp burning, and as a result, was prepared for the day that Sisera entered her tent. Jael encouraged Sisera not to be afraid as she covered him with a blanket and gave him milk, so he could rest. Jael had positioned herself as a watchman, so it is no surprise she was at the right place at the right time to take the life of Israel's enemy. While Sisera slept from exhaustion, Jael picked up a hammer and tent peg, driving the peg through his temple into the ground. Jael had only an instant to devise her plan, but I imagine she must have been laser-focused on her aim because she had only one chance to get it right.

What about you? What happens when you rise up like Deborah and Jael to become focused and fierce? How do you fight when you discover the enemy has taken territory in your life, marriage, children, or family? When you are focused and fierce, your lamp continually burns, making it impossible for the enemy to come into your fields to kill, steal, or destroy. Nothing will take you by surprise because your eyes scan the horizon as you answer the call to be a watchman over your family, community, and church. Isaiah 52:8 (NIV) tells of the joy that awaits the watchman: "Listen! Your watchmen lift up their voices, they shout joyfully together; for they will see with their own eyes when the Lord restores Zion." God wants to restore you, your marriage, children, and our country, but He needs people to rise up and become watchmen whose eyes are open to see the things God is doing and act upon what they see, much like a prophet.

I believe in the spiritual gift of prophecy, derived from the Greek word *propheteia* which relates to the declaration of God's divine inspiration and purposes. As Christians, I believe we are all called to be prophetic at times, meaning that we speak words of encouragement to a world that seems without hope. Being prophetic does not need to be weird—it simply means that you declare the Word of the Lord, bringing hope to the hopeless, healing to the sick, and repentance to the sinner. The world needs believers willing to speak an encouraging word from the Lord in a time of such incredible discouragement.

We can encourage people to repent without being judgmental about their past, "for all have sinned and fall short of the glory of God" (Romans 3:23, NIV). As we wake up and focus on our families, communities, and the world around us, we must do better when it comes to repentance. Repentance must be a daily practice. All of us, not just the ones who have made big mistakes, need to have our hearts right with Jesus. Joel 2:12 (NLT) says: "Turn to me now, while there is time. Give me your hearts. Come with fasting, weeping, and mourning."

I have learned to lean in and listen to what God is sharing with me so that in His perfect timing, I am prepared to share His Word when it is needed most, whenever God provides the opportunity. I often see prophetic pictures rather than just words. Not sure why, but it might be because I would rather see God's Word than hear it spoken. Plus, I have trouble remembering things. Maybe that is why God chooses to speak to me visually instead of verbally, because I may mess up the message. I believe God wants to speak to His people, if we would just learn to listen and focus on what God is doing. Remember, God spoke to Balaam through his donkey, so why would He not be able to speak through you?

Stay focused, my friend, when God wakes you up. Cling fiercely to God's calling as a watchman, careful that you do not lose sight of the vision He has given you for your life, marriage, career, family, church, and the world. Write down every vision, picture, word, and sound God gives you as you keep your lamp burning and wait upon the Lord to share the Word when He presents an opportunity. Habakkuk 2:2-3 (NLT) says:

"Write my answer plainly on tablets, so that a runner can carry the correct message to others. This vision is for a future time. It describes the end, and it will be

fulfilled. If it seems slow in coming, wait patiently,
for it will surely take place. It will not be delayed."

God is waiting for His watchmen and watchwomen to stay awake, so He can download pictures and words to describe to others what He wants us to see. You must do your part to remain focused on what God is calling you to do. Take your position and stand firm until God tells you to move. Stand firm with focus and fierceness against the schemes of the devil and refuse to let anyone take your vision away. Just look straight at your enemies and laser them with the power of the Holy Spirit. You are Superwoman!

05.

SHE USES HER VOICE

Has there ever been a time in your life when you had to stand up for something or someone? Perhaps you had to speak out against something with which you disagreed? I do not enjoy confrontation, and I struggle with speaking out, particularly if I know my words may cause tension or result in an argument. I was never the type of person who spoke out of turn or shared her thoughts openly in a crowd. You know the ones to whom I am referring—they dominate the conversation and expect everyone to just sit and listen.

What happens when you feel compelled to say something but are afraid to share your insight because of potential backlash or fear of the consequences when you speak your mind? I chicken out a lot of times from speaking up when I disagree with something. Unfortunately, my hesitation and overthinking the issue often prevent me from sharing my thoughts and opinions. I do not like it when I allow fear of confrontation to keep my mouth shut. When I got up and realized who I was in Christ, God took hold of my fears, and I discovered with a fierce focus that my voice matters. I had forgotten who I was, believing a lie that my voice did not matter because my opinions and wisdom were not good enough.

This lie that my voice didn't matter stems from my childhood. Until the age of seven, I was a thumb sucker. Because English is my second language, I stuck my thumb in my mouth every time I did not want to speak for fear that I would not use English properly. That little lie of inadequacy led to a greater lie: the fear of shame. I did not want to be shamed by peers, so I chose not to speak up.

Isn't it strange how the enemy wants to silence our voices? He will entice you to put your thumb in your mouth to try and keep you silent from speaking up, whether it is fear of saying the wrong words or shame of the way others will react to your words. We all want to sound intelligent and wise and use our words correctly when we share our thoughts. No one wants to sound dumb or be accused of being wrong. At one time or another, all of us have experienced being teased, corrected, or even shamed when we finally got up and shared our thoughts, ideas, and vision. The enemy uses those experiences as reminders to intimidate us into shutting our mouths, using whatever means necessary to convince us that our voice does not matter.

Moses was someone who felt inadequate when God called him to speak to Pharoah on behalf of the Israelites. In Exodus 3:11 (NIV), Moses argued with God:

> *"Who am I, that I should go to Pharaoh and*
> *bring the Israelites out of Egypt?"*

Despite God's assurances, Moses continued to express his fears.

> *"What if they do not believe me or listen to my*
> *voice? For they may say, 'The LORD has not*
> *appeared to you'" (Exodus 4:1, BSB).*

No doubt the enemy spoke lies of intimidation to Moses as he continued:

"I have never been eloquent, neither in the past nor since You have spoken to Your servant, for I am slow of speech and tongue" (Exodus 4:10, NIV).

While I am sure Pharoah must have been a terrifying figure to the captive Israelites, God's response is the same for you and me:

"Who gave man his mouth? Or who makes the mute or the deaf sighted or the blind? Is it not I, the Lord? Now go! I will help you as you speak, and I will teach you what to say" (Exodus 4:11-12, BSB).

I first met international speaker, best-selling author, and personal friend, John Bevere, at our leadership conference many years ago. I can still vividly recall both of his timely delivered messages: "The Extraordinary Life" and "Overcoming Intimidation." Hey, if I can still remember those messages all these years later, they must have been really good! I mean, how many of us can say we remember the message from last week's church teaching? His message on intimidation resonated with me because I never really thought I had a problem with insecurity. Of course, it is usually when you do not think you have a problem that you later realize you actually do—you just have not admitted it to yourself yet.

At the conclusion of his message, John posed a question: "How many of you want to be set free from intimidation? If you do, I need you to stand up." Let me first begin by saying that God was already working on my heart at the end of John's first message. By the time I heard the message on overcoming intimidation, God had softened my heart so much that I was ready for Him to change me from the inside out. However, moments like these scare me. After all, I am a pastor's wife. If people see me stand, they will immediately know my personal struggles. Nevertheless, I wanted healing and deliverance, so I made the decision to stand.

To my surprise, about 90 percent of the people in the room stood up too. John prayed for us; then, he told us we needed to shout as loud as we could. I was stunned. I could understand shouting at a concert or a sports game, but at church? I had never done anything like this before in a public place of worship. Thank God I was not alone because 90 percent of the people in that room were about to shout at the same time. On the count of three, nearly everyone in attendance shouted at the top of their lungs. Boy, did it feel good! We kept shouting until we felt God begin to release the tension, anxiety, and fear that had held us in bondage for so long—until we let go of the enemy's intimidation over our voices. As awkward as it was to shout in public, this simple act of obedience empowered me to become vulnerable with God and with the people in the room. We all shared a moment together that forever changed our lives.

That conference transformed my life. It was the moment that I decided to get up and refuse to allow people to intimidate me into silencing my voice. It was the moment I realized who gave me my voice. I discovered, like Moses, that God is the One who has given me my mouth, who will help me as I speak, and who will teach me what I should say. I have a voice, and my voice was given to me by an almighty and creative God. I realized that it was time to stop pleasing people with my words and start pleasing God by using my voice.

One of the greatest weaknesses of intimidated people is that they are so busy trying to please people that they fail to recognize God is the One they need to be pleasing. Who is holding back your voice? How long has the enemy silenced your voice to speak or sing? Are you tired of being contained, strapped, fearful, or stuck—always shying away from sharing what is truly on your mind or your heart? This fear can shut us up for a long time, even permanently if we let it. God desires for each of you to use your voice; it is meant to be heard! He has given us a voice to use for this generation, and we will not be silenced by the enemy.

Joshua commands his people in Joshua 6 to shout. What was the purpose of this shouting? It was to shatter enemy walls, so the Israelites could access new territory and gain ground that the enemy had occupied. If the people had failed to use their voices, the walls would not have come down. Their voices determined their victory. Joshua 6:20 (NIV) says this:

> *"When the trumpets sounded, the army shouted, and at the sound of the trumpet, when the men gave a loud shout, the wall collapsed; so everyone charged straight in, and they took the city."*

When the children of God speak, our voice has authority given to us by the Holy Spirit. Upon whose authority are you relying when you use your voice? Your voice can shatter a glass and change the mood of any atmosphere. Is it because you are an eloquent and gifted speaker? Perhaps. But even a speaker like Moses has power and authority when he speaks because God gives the words to say. As you lift your voice in a triumphant noise, it changes the atmosphere of the room, in your heart, and in your thoughts. I never knew I had authority in my voice, but once I found it, I have never stopped using it. I use it when I sing. I use it whenever I see unrighteousness happening around me. I use it when I sense the devil is prowling around and looking for someone to devour. I use my voice especially as I pray.

Like 1 Corinthians 14:15 encourages us to do, I pray with my spirit in my spiritual language God has given me while also praying with my understanding. Rather than words of doubt—"if, maybe, could you, can you, would you,"—I pray with fighting words because I have the authority of Jesus in my voice. You must instead use words like "it shall be, I command, I declare, I take authority over, I refuse to allow" ending your prayer "in the name of Jesus." By what authority do we use the name of Jesus when we speak? Jesus Himself has given us authority as stated in Matthew 28:18 (NIV):

*"Then Jesus came to them and said, "All authority
in heaven and on earth has been given to me."*

In Matthew 10:1 (NIV), Jesus "called his twelve disciples to Him and gave them authority to drive out impure spirits and to heal every disease and sickness." Jesus also says that we will do greater things after He leaves this earth in John 14:12 (NIV):

"Very truly I tell you, whoever believes in me will do the works I have been doing, and they will do even greater things than these, because I am going to the Father."

If you are wondering if you can use His authority over your situation when you speak, then receive His words right now. Stop second-guessing yourself when you pray aloud and use your voice. Pray to the heavens and pray like it shall be done in heaven and on earth. Take back your voice from the enemy and begin using it now to sing, shout, and worship Jesus with all your heart, mind, and soul. Throw off the enemy's intimidation, get up, and start using your voice. Use your voice to give God the praise He deserves.

Psalm 98:4-9 (NKJV) reads:

Shout joyfully to the Lord, all the earth;
Break forth in song, rejoice, and sing praises.
Sing to the Lord with the harp,
With the harp and the sound of a psalm,
With trumpets and the sound of a horn;
Shout joyfully before the Lord, the King.
Let the sea roar, and all its fullness,
The world and those who dwell in it;
Let the rivers clap their hands;
Let the hills be joyful together
before the Lord,
For He is coming to judge the earth.
With righteousness He shall judge the world,
And the peoples with equity.

The Bible is filled with incredible examples of how Jesus used His voice to set in motion the miraculous. A girl was restored to life when her father, Jairus, begged Jesus to come and heal his daughter from her illness. Although they received the tragic news that this precious child had died while they were on the way to her home, Jesus told Jairus to only believe and not be afraid. Upon reaching the home, Jesus took the father and mother of the girl as well as Peter, James, and John to the room where the girl was lying.

Then He took the child by the hand, and said to her, "Talitha, cumi," which translated,

> *"Little girl, I say to you, arise!" Immediately the girl arose and walked, for she was twelve years of age. And they were overcome with great amazement.* —Mark 5:41–42 (NKJV)

In this instance, Jesus was a man of few words, but when He spoke just six of them, the power and authority in His voice were enough to raise a dead little girl to life. This, my friend, is the same power and authority Jesus gives to each one of His followers. I cannot stress enough to you how much authority we have behind our words when we pray or speak the words God gives us for one another. When we pray and speak, we must believe God is able to accomplish the impossible. The key word is *believe*. You must believe when you ask.

Do not be afraid to speak with authority and ask God for anything that aligns with His will because God is more than able to do the miraculous. Just look at the life of Joshua who asked God to make the sun stand still because he needed more daylight to win the battle. If God can make the sun stand still for Joshua, just think of what He can do for you if you use your voice to ask. The account is written in Joshua 10:12-14 (NIV):

On the day the Lord gave the Amorites over to Israel, Joshua said to the Lord in the presence of Israel: "Sun, stand still over Gibeon, and you, moon, over the Valley of Aijalon." So the sun stood still, and the moon stopped, till the nation avenged itself on its enemies, as it is written in the Book of Jashar. The sun stopped in the middle of the sky and delayed going down about a full day. There has never been a day like it before or since, a day when the Lord listened to a human being. Surely the Lord was fighting for Israel!

Remember the story of Lazarus in John 11? Mary asked Jesus to heal her brother Lazarus who had fallen ill and subsequently died. He remained in the tomb for a while until Jesus was finally able to make His way to Lazarus. Although Jesus has the power even over death, I think he must have been frustrated over the lack of faith he witnessed when he arrived at the tomb. Jesus said to her,

Did I not say to you that if you would believe you would see the glory of God?" Then they took away the stone from the place where the dead man was lying. And Jesus lifted up His eyes and said, "Father, I thank You that You have heard Me. And I know that You always hear Me, but because of the people who are standing by, I said this, that they may believe that You sent Me." Now when He had said these things, He cried with a loud voice, "Lazarus, come forth!" And he who had died came out bound hand and foot with graveclothes, and his face was wrapped with a cloth. Jesus said to them, "Loose him, and let him go."
—*John 11:40-43 (NKJV)*

Three powerful words were shouted in a loud voice that day, yet the power behind them shook the foundations of the grave and restored to life that which death had stolen. It was not the words but the power and authority behind the voice—the same voice that God has given to each of His children. My friend, when you are awake and realize the authority you have in your voice, you will need to shout louder in your praises and prayers. Pray and worship aloud and believe with all your heart in what you say. Remove the doubt that fills your heart and mind by speaking life and hope rather than death and pain.

I know it is not easy to use your voice and shout away the enemy's intimidation, particularly when you go through a rough time in your marriage, family, or work or even the challenges we face with our nation. We are more than conquerors, and we serve a God who desires for us to wake up and walk with strength and courage. Let our voices echo through the walls and through every crevice on this planet as we proclaim the name of Jesus and watch the miraculous unfold.

What happens when you find your voice? What will you do when you finally get up and realize that you have allowed your voice to be influenced by negative and doubtful thoughts? What words are you putting into the atmosphere? Are they words of hope or words of fear? What songs are you singing over your life? Would the banner over your life shout out, "I am who God says I am!" or would it scream, "I am who the enemy says I am"? Do not let your circumstances reflect or direct your words and your praise. Let God's Word reflect and direct your words and praise over your circumstance.

Once I found my voice, I had to use it in my personal prayer time and as I pray for others. I believe God has anointed me to pray with authority over couples who are having difficulty conceiving a baby. God allowed me to go through a long season of infertility with my youngest daughter, Charis. I could not understand why I was having such a challenging time since I had already given birth to my middle child, Bekah. It took nine years to conceive another child. The struggle was real, and it was probably the most difficult season of my faith journey. However, I am so blessed to have gone through it because it allowed me to lean on God and trust Him throughout the entire process.

It is not easy when you keep praying and believing with anticipation for the doctor to say, "You're pregnant," only to be disappointed month after month and year after year. Mike and I went through seven artificial inseminations and none worked. I endured so much during this journey, from removing scar tissue from endometriosis I had developed over the years to the removal of my thyroid because I discovered I was afflicted with Graves' disease. I could have quit along the journey, but I kept believing and used my voice to begin declaring victory over my womb, my husband's sperm count, the size of my eggs, that my fallopian tubes would be wide open . . . you name it, I prayed in faith for it.

I know this seems very detailed, but we need to be specific when we use our voices in prayer. Once I found my voice, it transformed the way I prayed because I recognized I had to take authority over my body and make it submit to the authority of Jesus. I believe what God commands Adam and Eve in Genesis 1:22 (NLT) still applies today:

"Be fruitful and multiply."

That is what I held onto for nine years until I conceived Charis. So, when I pray for other couples now, I refuse to just pray, "God give them a baby." I pray by laying my hands over the woman's womb and taking authority over the eggs, fallopian tubes, and hormones and that her ovaries would come into alignment with her body to produce a baby.

I also pray for the husband (Do not worry; I do not lay hands on his organs but on his shoulders!) in case you were wondering. I pray for the husband's sperm to be Olympic swimmers, so they can swim fast and dissect the strongest grade A egg. I also pray for the multiplication of sperm as well as a clear passage for the sperm to swim out in the name of Jesus. That is how you take authority! You speak to the mountain by name and declare over it what it should be doing. Whatever your situation is, use your voice and know that in the mighty name of Jesus you have authority to take dominion over every situation. Keep worship at the forefront of your battle. You need to know who is in charge.

In Acts 16, Paul and Silas cast out a demonic spirit from a female slave who brought in considerable profit to her owners as a fortune teller. Although the woman was set free from tormenting spirits, her owners became angry at their loss of income and brought Paul and Silas before the Roman magistrates, and accused them of causing an uproar throughout the city. The magistrates flogged Paul and Silas and threw them in prison:

> *About midnight Paul and Silas were praying and singing hymns to God, and the other prisoners were listening to them. Suddenly there was such a violent earthquake that the foundations of the prison were shaken. At once all the prison doors flew open, and everyone's chains came loose.* —*Acts 16:25-26 (NIV)*

Worship breaks chains, opens doors and sets prisoners free. Worship shifts the atmosphere so that His children fight from a place of victory. Is it any wonder that King Jehoshaphat positioned the worshipers at the front of the battle lines to set in motion the victory? Second Chronicles 20:21-22 (NIV) tell the story:

After consulting the people, Jehoshaphat appointed men to sing to the Lord and to praise him for the splendor of his holiness as they went out at the head of the army, saying: "Give thanks to the Lord, for his love endures forever." As they began to sing and praise, the Lord set ambushes against the men of Ammon and Moab and Mount Seir who were invading Judah, and they were defeated.

God began to move while the people worshiped! If you are a worshiper of God, sing and shout out praises in a loud voice. I love it when worship leaders lead with authority because they are frontline warriors that lead us into battle. We are all in a battle and must use our voices to put on our worship because worship leads to victory. Can I propose that worship leaders need to remember where their authority comes from? Use your voices to walk in boldness and lead us into battle with the songs that wake us up and get us through the battles. I call these worship songs our fight songs. We need more fight songs than songs that simply make us happy and lull us back to sleep.

What is your fight song? You must have a playlist on your phone that you listen to that will help you with your faith. I love listening to William McDowell, Belonging Co, Elevation Worship, and so many other artists that sing declarative songs. What is a declarative song? It is a song with authoritative lyrics that speak of hope and life to show you what God can do in your situation and remind you who He is. What is that song or scripture you go back to when you need to remain steadfast and stay awake? It is time to use your voice and shout louder than ever before, so you break through the enemy's intimidation on your way to your breakthrough.

Find your voice and know that God gave you that voice to use. God has empowered you to fight all the battles you will face today and will face tomorrow. The enemy will do his best to silence you, but never shy away from the voice God gave you. He knows what your voice can do in any battle. He even knows there is victory in worship because he was once a worship leader in Heaven. He led one of the most amazing worship teams, but then he lost it all when his worship became about him rather than about God.

It is time to get up! Stay wide awake and shout louder with God's authority over your life, health, marriage, children, finances—everything. I want the enemy to say this about you, "Oh Crap, She's Up!" The enemy hears you loud and clear because you are fully awake, no longer sitting in silence but using your voice with full authority and faith! Way to go, my friend. Keep shouting and believing what God says about you. Believe for God's best in your life.

When you need just a little more faith to believe the impossible, pray this prayer over your life:

Jesus, I come to You with thanksgiving, for You are my God, and I am Your daughter. By the power of the Holy Spirit, I declare healing, provision, wisdom, strategies, knowledge, and guidance over my situation. I believe You hear my prayers, and I declare Your will be done in my life. I proclaim that Your Word over my life will bring restoration, healing, and anointing. Thank You, Jesus, for what You are about to do in me and through me in Jesus' name. Amen.

CONCLUSION: SHE'S YIELDED TO GOD'S SPIRIT

I've been listening to the beautiful worship song "Just to Be Close to You" by CeCe Winans recently. It speaks of our desire to be close to Jesus, and it got me thinking. Do you desire to be with Jesus? Do you desire His presence? Do you desire to follow Him? When you're yielded to His Spirit, it comes from a place of desiring more of Jesus in your life. Our desires dictate our priorities in life. Sometimes, we drift away from our desire for God because our desires shift from more of Him to more of an idol. An idol is anything besides God that takes the place of God in your life. It could be your career, children, money, fame, or power. God said in Deuteronomy 4:23 (NLT):

*"So be careful not to forget the covenant that the
Lord your God made with you, and not to make
for yourselves an idol in the form of anything
that the Lord your God has forbidden you."*

Yielding to God's Spirit means desiring and prioritizing Him above all else.

Now that you are up and have finally found your voice, what happens next? You must be yielded to God's Spirit. Ephesians 5:18 (NIV) stresses:

"Be filled with the Spirit."

Why is it important to be filled with the Spirit? When you are filled with the Spirit, you will not be tempted to lay your head back on your comfy pillow and fall back to sleep. The Holy Spirit will keep you from taking Satan's sleeping pills or allowing the enemy to lull you back to sleep with any more of his lullabies. When you are Spirit-filled, you will refuse to sit comfortably in your Lazy Boy chair and remain complacent with life. Instead, there is nothing that will keep you distant from God because you will fight for your time with Jesus. How many of us have allowed distractions, busy schedules, or our need for sleep to get in the way of our time with Jesus?

As I was doing my devotions a while back, God showed me a picture of a gas tank. At that moment, I felt God was saying that the tank was a representation of our souls, and many of us have been running on empty or half-filled. We know we should fill our tanks to full capacity, but oftentimes we only put in the bare minimum at the gas station: five or ten dollars as needed just to get us to the next destination. God showed me that He wants to fill our tanks to the fullest! When the tank starts to get empty, we need to go to Him to fill our souls back up. We don't want to run on empty but with a full tank of His Spirit. The only way to have a full tank is to be in His presence and to feed on His Word.

It is important that you do not let the distractions and the busyness of routines prevent you from spending time with the Lord. What makes you get up in the morning? Even more importantly, what makes you get on your knees every morning? One of the surest practices to ensure your life is yielded to the Spirit is prayer. How can you experience victory through tough and difficult seasons as you spiritually fight for your marriage, children, finances, relationships, business, and sanity? It is only through prayer! It begins by falling on your knees every morning and yielding yourself to the presence of Jesus and His Holy Spirit.

I mentioned this quote at the very beginning of this book: "Be the kind of woman that when your feet hit the floor each morning, the devil says, 'OH CRAP, SHE'S UP!'" Satan does not like it when you are finally up and aware of what is happening to you or the circumstances surrounding you. I can just see Satan joyfully watching you spiritually sleep day in and day out as you go through your busy day, struggling to find time to fit Jesus into your schedule. But whenever the enemy sees you get up and hit that floor, he screams in agony, "Oh, no, she is going to get on her knees and pray! SHE'S UP!"

Satan thinks he has you in the palm of his hand, but when you make the decision to get up and yield to God's Spirit as you pray, he is terrified of you. Why? Because the enemy knows that when you work together with God, miracles and healing begin to unfold in your life. Satan knows the battles are won through prayer, so he will do everything in his power to keep you from it. He would much rather see you slumbering in a catatonic state, performing routine after routine but never waking up to yield to God's Spirit and pray for breakthroughs. I have seen so many people, including myself, fall back to sleep and return to the old routine of being too busy or too distracted with jobs or kids to spend time on their knees in prayer. Sadly, that is how you grow distant from God. It is always a tell-tale sign for me when I fail to spend time with Jesus. I become impatient with people, controlling, irritable, and unkind. You must be thinking, "Not Lisa Kai!" But oh, yes! Just ask my family. Then again, don't ask them. They may exaggerate.

It grieves the Holy Spirit when we do not make time to spend time with Him in the Word and in prayer. Where do you go to spend time with Jesus? It is important that you find a place where there are no distractions, and you can actually talk with Him without interruption. My walks alone with Jesus on the beach in beautiful Kailua, Hawai'i, where I reside, is one of the places I can be fully alone without distractions. What a place to be alone with Jesus, huh? I am so blessed to be able to drive just five minutes down the road to the beach and walk with a Starbucks Chai Tea Latte and my AirPods as I listen to worship music and yield to the Holy Spirit.

As I am walking and worshiping, I try to focus on what God wants to say to me and then I find a place to sit and pray aloud in my spiritual language, just praising Him and thanking Him for who He is and what He has done for me and my family. There is no better place to sit and be alone with God than the beach with the ocean as my view. Often, when I spend time with God, I feel like I am bursting on the inside, ready to release the tension I feel within my spirit and flesh by yelling and screaming away my anxiety, stress, fears, and concerns. When I spend these moments with Jesus, I am in a safe place that gives me the freedom to release all my cares and leave my burdens at the foot of the cross.

When we are fully awake and yielded to God's Spirit, we will release our burdens to God because that is what He wants us to do. Psalm 55:22 (NLT) encourages us:

> *"Give your burdens to the Lord, and he will take care of you. He will not permit the godly to slip and fall." As you continue to yield to God, you will learn to stay awake and alert without falling into temptation that leads to sin. In fact, the more time you spend with Him, the more awake you will be.*

Why is this message so important for you and me? Why is it so crucial that you and I get up and yield to God's Spirit? It is because we have been slacking on the job for far too long. We do not understand who we are and how capable we are. We are God's children, and we have the power of the Holy Spirit living inside of us to make a difference on earth. God is calling us to change the world for Christ, but it must begin with our very own households. Once we fight for our marriage and children, we must fight for our communities so that people come to know Jesus. We must fight for our churches, so they remain open and can continue meeting the needs of a hurting world. We cannot allow the enemy to take any more territory than he already has, especially during this pandemic.

The enemy is well aware that Jesus will return soon, so he is working overtime to make certain we never wake up. But the minute you make the decision to open your eyes and turn off the snooze button, Satan shrieks, "OH CRAP, SHE'S UP!" Oh Crap, Lisa's UP! Oh Crap, Bekah is UP! The enemy shouts, "Oh Crap, Charis, Katy, Lillia, Kai, Selah, Isabelle, Aria, Sierra, and so many more that I could name ... are all UP!" Can Satan say that about you? Is he afraid of you? When you are fully awake, the answer is yes. Is he afraid that you will figure out the truth about yourself, speak up, and rebuke the lies he tells you about your purpose and who you are? The answer is a resounding yes.

The devil doesn't care if you go to church or read your
Bible, as long as you don't apply it to your life.
—Unknown

As your friend, I need you to wake up! Even if I have to slap you to get you up, I will. There are so many sisters and brothers on the frontlines battling it out with Satan who are exhausted and need you to come alongside them to do the same. We are in this battle together, and nothing will be won without a battle. We must deal with the distractions of life, mundane routines, and sin that so easily trip us up and make us want to go back to sleep. We have to finish this race that God has for us. We must finish! Hebrews 12:1-2 (NLT) says:

Therefore, since we are surrounded by such a huge
crowd of witnesses to the life of faith, let us strip off
every weight that slows us down, especially the sin that
so easily trips us up. And let us run with endurance the

race God has set before us. We do this by keeping our eyes on Jesus, the champion who initiates and perfects our faith. Because of the joy awaiting him, he endured the cross, disregarding its shame. Now he is seated in the place of honor beside God's throne.

As we begin to wake up and yield to God's Spirit, we become empowered to advance the Kingdom as a believer of Jesus Christ and love one another as Jesus loves. His Spirit gives us the ability to forgive and have mercy on one another—to show kindness and compassion.

Ephesian 3:14-21(NIV) says:

For this reason I kneel before the Father, from whom every family in heaven and on earth derives its name. I pray that out of his glorious riches he may strengthen you with power through his Spirit in your inner being, so that Christ may dwell in your hearts through faith. And I pray that you, being rooted and established in love, may have power, together with all the Lord's holy people, to grasp how wide and long and high and deep is the love of Christ, and to know this love that surpasses knowledge—that you may be filled to the measure of all the fullness of God.

Now to him who is able to do immeasurably more than all we ask or imagine, according to his power that is at work within us, to him be glory in the church and in Christ Jesus throughout all generations, for ever and ever! Amen.

God is the Alpha and the Omega, the Beginning and the End. He created the earth and everything in it, but one day everything will be gone. I believe we are living in "the middle." I'm not sure what part of the middle, but it is not the end yet because you are still reading this book. Rest assured that God is well aware of everything happening on earth and every detail of what is happening in your life because God knows you better than you know yourself. God's power is working in you and is able to do immeasurably more than your mind can comprehend. He has gifted you with spiritual gifts unique to you and considers you useful, important, acceptable, smart, beautiful, and so loved. The time to yield your life to Him is now. It is time to wake up!

When Jesus raised Lazarus from the dead, He explained, "Our friend Lazarus has fallen asleep; but I am going there to wake him up" (John 11:11, NIV). Jesus is saying the same thing to you: "I am going to wake you up." When He does, will you keep your eyes open this time or hit the snooze button? My friends, will you join me along with thousands of women across the globe as we accelerate the coming of God's Kingdom? Together, I believe we can change the world. Let's all wake up!

I love you, and I believe the best is yet to come for you and for me. There is a battle ahead, and we need to be ready with our knees to the floor and swords at our side as we yield to the Spirit. We can do nothing without Him. Once you are awake, find a local Christian community where you can plant your roots and grow. Pray about where you can use your gifts and talents to serve in the local church, whether it be working with children, serving on worship, or greeting visitors. Use your voice to speak out as the Holy Spirit leads, in your families, your workplace, and in your local, state, and global communities.

Now that you are awake, here's what I want you to do:

01. Tell someone! Whether it's your husband, best friend, or pastor, tell them what God is showing you, and have them pray with you. When I first got the wake-up call at a conference, I hesitated to tell anyone for fear I may have heard wrong. It wasn't until my husband asked to hear all that God had shown me that

I was able to share with him. That was the start of my awakening. So, go and tell someone for accountability, and allow them to walk with you along your journey.

02. Dive into the Word, and worship like crazy! This will keep you awake! Don't let up on your thankfulness of Jesus, and continue to remind yourself who He is. Learn to open up your heart, and let Him come and minister to you to give you boldness and strength for the days ahead.

03. Get into a community! You find strength in community by getting involved in people's lives. Form friendships with women, learn to trust them, and allow them into your life. A form of waking up is being real with yourself and with others. So, just as you seek authentic friends, be authentic as well. Go and visit that connect group or Bible study, and just say yes. Be an answer to the problems of this world! Stop complaining about what's happening in the world, and get involved in your government and community. Volunteer with outreaches, give back, and be a part of the committees that can make good decisions for your children, your state, and your country. Go and run for governor or even to be the President of the

United States. We need more men and women to hold public office, so they can be the voice for God. You have more in you than you know. Go, and use what's in your hand.

04. Wake up your sister! Now that you're awake, it's time for you to be someone else's wake-up call! Don't shrink back. We need strong, fearless, and wise people to lead at such a time as this. God didn't wake you up for nothing. He has an assignment for you now, not later!

So, who is with me? Are you letting your season or day-to-day circumstances lull you into becoming unaware of what God is up to? Will you be like Peter in the Garden of Gethsemane and struggle to keep your eyes open, unprepared for the extraordinary because you are stuck in the mundane of what you think is just an ordinary day? You can wait for the alarm to wake you up, tempted by the snooze that beckons you to grab just a few more minutes of slumber, or you can make the decision today to wake yourself up and stay awake, watching and waiting with great expectation.

I do not want to do battle without you by my side. We need each other to fight the battles that rage against us because the enemy is strong, but God is much stronger.

It is time to shut the door on the enemy and sound the alarm as we wake up and realize Satan is attacking our marriages, children, and everything that we have. The Holy Spirit is shaking you right now, and he will not stop until you wake up. I will not stop until you wake up. I am fighting for you and with you and refuse to let the devil put you back to sleep. Come on, let's go and get our jobs done for the Kingdom! Let us force the enemy into crying out all over the world, "Oh crap, She's finally UP! And once you are awake, make certain to wake up others around you and keep them from falling back to sleep. Can I count on you? I love you and am praying that God will reveal all things within your spirit, so you may yield to Him today, tomorrow, and always.